YOU ARE

LOVED

BY A FATHER

D1553845

YOU ARE

LOVED

BY A FATHER

Andrew Enos

ABUNDANT HARVEST
PUBLISHING

Editing/Formatting: Erik V. Sahakian
Cover Design/Layout: Andrew Enos
Cover Photo: Rolly Ladd

Library of Congress Control Number: 2019911484

ISBN 978-1-7327173-8-1
First Printing: December 2019

FOR INFORMATION CONTACT:

Abundant Harvest Publishing
35145 Oak Glen Rd
Yucaipa, CA 92399
www.abundantharvestpublishing.com

Printed in the United States of America

This book is dedicated to my beautiful wife, Laura, and our six beautiful children: Elijah, Harper, India, Scout, Augie, and our heaven-baby, Cove. Thank you all for giving me a greater glimpse of our Father's heart.
1-4-3-2-4-7

CONTENTS

FOREWORD

All throughout the Bible, we find reference after reference to God being a father. It's such a recurring theme that you come to understand that God is wanting to communicate something really important to us.

We can often think of God in other ways such as God the righteous judge, or God the eternal king, etc. All of which are true! But the primary image that Jesus wants us to understand is that God is our Father.

We get a clear picture of that when Jesus taught His disciples to address God, when we pray, with these very words, "Our Father in heaven." Paul would even go on to say later in the epistles that the Holy Spirit works in us so we cry out, "Abba, Father."

I've had the privilege of knowing Andrew Enos for some years now and he is passionate about living in light of the reality that God is a faithful father. Andrew does such a great job of communicating that through his life, ministry, and attitude and really captures it well in this easy to read book.

As you read this book, you will find yourself encouraged and reminded to live in light of this beautiful truth as well, as Andrew simply and skillfully applies it to our lives as followers of Jesus.

Scott Cunningham

Worship Pastor, Calvary Chapel Costa Mesa

PART ONE:

YOU ARE

LOVED

UNDERSTANDING YOUR PURPOSE, IDENTITY, AND THE COMMUNITY THAT YOU WERE CREATED FOR

CHAPTER ONE:

THE INCEPTION OF COMMUNITY

I think the best place to begin this book is back where everything began. See, I have come to understand that many of the issues that we face in life, Christian or not, can be traced back to a lack of understanding of one major theme— God's love for us.

Perhaps you grew up like I did, singing, "Jesus loves me, this I know, for the Bible tells me so." Those words hold great truth and depth, yet somehow they can become so familiar that they get buried beneath all the lies that compile throughout our lives.

These days, from a young age, the lie is being imposed upon children that they came from nothing, and that through some cosmic accident mankind was eventually brought to be. It's thought that not only did we come from nothing, but we're going nowhere in the end. I believe this is one of the main reasons that we've seen such hopeless generations lately.

It would seem the lie of the devil has become the loudest voice, and sometimes, if we're honest, we live as though we believe it. We can say that we know we were created for a purpose, all the while living without a true and simple understanding of God's love for us. His purpose and plan for mankind started with His love.

Here's the truth…are you ready for it?

You are not a mistake. You are not an accident. Your story began in the heart of God.

You are loved.

Recently, one of my close friends brought up a really good point when we were discussing our relationship with God. He said, "We often try to sell the Gospel to the world as some sort of 'get out of hell free' card…but in doing so we miss out on the opportunity to explain God's desire for community with us."

He is absolutely right. God's desire for a relationship with mankind quite literally goes all the way back to the inception of time and space. The purpose for creation—the universe, earth, and all that dwells within it—was simply for the purpose of God and man coexisting in eternal fellowship and community.

Genesis 1:26 says, "Then God said, 'Let Us make man in Our image, according to Our likeness.'" That name in Hebrew for God is *elohim*, which is a plural name for God. In this verse we get to see the fellowship of the Godhead inviting humanity into the oneness of the Father, Son, and Holy Spirit.

God Himself is in constant fellowship among the three persons that make up the Trinity.

When God said, "according to Our likeness," He was specifying that humans would have an innate desire for relationships. Think about that: your desire for friendships, marriage, children, and fellowship are not simply desires; they are needs. You were built for community with God and with others.

The fact that we were built for eternity with our Creator is truly humbling. God created us to spend forever with Him because He loves us. It's tragic to think that there will be some people who will choose to spend their eternity apart from the One who made them, because ultimately that's why we exist. Fellowship and community on this side of eternity have the purpose of equipping us for heaven where we'll be together, united by the blood of Jesus forevermore.

Community started in the heart of God and will continue throughout the duration of eternity. We should desire community with our Lord because He desired it with us first.

Allow this truth to sink in and humble you in this moment: the author of life and all creation loves you and longs to have fellowship with you. Yes, this is true of everyone that He has ever created, but His desire is not just accumulative, it's direct—He loves you.

God, Elohim, Jehovah, the Messiah (insert amazing name for Him here) desires to have a one-on-one constant relationship with you. He wants to help you, He wants to lead you, and He wants to be loved by you.

THE GOSPEL: DIVINE INTERVENTION

When sin entered the picture it did more than kick Adam and Eve out of the garden, it created disunity between God and man. The Lord, in His infinite perfection, could not be joined together with man in a sinful and imperfect state. That combination would never work. Just like water and oil, God and sin will never mix.

God was not surprised by man's sin, that's why the plan of salvation was set into motion. Where man caused the divide, the Lord brought the divine intervention. It's the Gospel!

Jesus, the one and only Son of God, was not just sent to save us from hell, He was sent because of the love of the Father and Christ's desire to spend eternity with His bride (His church).

The blood of Jesus conveys us into a state of spiritual cleanliness that enables a fellowship that was previously obstructed by sin. The restoration of garden-like communion is the focal point of the Gospel. It's good news to all who believe and receive.

Even down to the moment when Jesus became our sin upon the cross, as the Father could not look upon the sin that His Son had borne, it would appear for that brief moment in history that the Son of God, a member of the triune Godhead, was exiled from the union that had existed throughout eternity, and the kicker is that it was all done for love's sake. He who knew no sin became sin for us. Why? Because He loves us and wanted to reconcile us back into fellowship with the Father.

We should find great hope in the fact that heaven is presented as an option to us, even though we were born into the fallen state of this world. His love stops short of no one.

One of the greatest passages on the broad love of Jesus is Second Peter 3:9, which states, "The Lord is not slack concerning His promise, as some count slackness, but is longsuffering toward us, not willing that any should perish but that all should come to repentance."

What amazing grace...that a wretch like me can be saved.

PICTURES FOR US TO FOLLOW

Because our God is so relational, He has graciously granted us living pictures, glimpses of His character, and the opportunity to see life through His eyes. They are all throughout His Word.

In the garden, He gave us the picture of marriage with Adam and Eve. Marriage is a picture of Christ and His church. We have biblical principles to live by for the husband and the wife. To husbands, Paul says, "Love your wives, just as Christ also loved the church and gave Himself for her." And to the wives, he says, "Submit to your own husbands, as to the Lord." Marriage helps us understand the teamwork between husband and wife to make up a living picture of Christ and His bride.

In this book we're going to focus on the picture of the Father and His children. There are many references in the Bible to God being the Father, Jesus being the Son, and us who are saved being children of God. Arguably one of the most popularly memorized verses is John 3:16, "For God so loved the world that He gave His only begotten Son, that whoever believes in Him should not perish but have everlasting life."

It was from the loving heart of a Father that the Son was sent so that we can be saved. This is the reason that we worship, this is the reason that we serve, and this is the reason that we seek a relational walk with Christ.

From a young age, I knew that God is called our "Father," but it didn't hold nearly as much weight in my heart as it does now. Now that I'm married and a father myself, this truth helps me understand more about the heart of God. What once was a cool title for God is currently a great gift to my relationship with Him.

On a daily basis, my heavenly Father continues to unveil His heart to me by way of experience as a father to my own children.

In the chapters that follow, we will explore some of the pictures that we find in the scriptures that will help us understand more about God, more about ourselves, and that will prayerfully drive us into a deeper life of worship with a Father who cherishes the relationship He has with His children.

CHAPTER TWO:

MORE THAN A SONG

I've had the privilege of serving in the area of worship in various forms at a variety of different churches for the past sixteen years. I feel like I'm just getting started, but I also feel like the Lord has allowed me to face many different trials in ministry at a young age to shape the way that I view worship and ministry.

When I was a child, I encountered difficulties in the church that became a deterrent for me. By the time I was approaching high school, I was wounded and I let the flaws of man shape my view of the church. At the time, I longed for a way out of that valley, but on this side of it I'm grateful because it has helped to shape my life of worship.

I have watched throughout the years how worship can easily be passed off as the time that we sing songs before the message, and it's limited to when we're in a church building. I think that if we carry that mindset into our walks with God, it can be dangerous and stifling to our spiritual growth.

Worship is one of the most unifying things that we can experience spiritually on this side of heaven. That's because it's an earthly practice of an eternal activity.

The term "worship" these days is often associated with a genre of music and not a condition of the heart, and that is not at all representative of the origin of that word.

The word *shachah* that is translated "worship" in the Old Testament literally speaks of one bowing down in the presence of someone who is superior to them.

You see, worship is about so much more than a song...it's a state of heart that is relentlessly bowed in reverence to the One who reigns in perfect love and justice.

In my personal walk with my heavenly Father, I've come to understand worship as a tool that He uses to get me through various seasons in life. Through valleys, worship keeps me hopeful, and on mountaintops it keeps me humble. Worship is the exaltation of the only One who deserves it every moment, and with every breath.

Maybe you don't see yourself as being much of a worshiper. You may not like singing or lifting your hands, but I hope that you're encouraged with the reality of the place that worship has in your eternal destiny and the benefits that it has on this side of heaven.

I am constantly made aware of the fact that worship is about so much more than just a song. It's about a walk…walking with the One who has conveyed us from darkness into His marvelous light, the One who has adopted us into His family, the One who calls you son or daughter.

THE SYMMETRY OF WORSHIP & PRAYER

As far as I can tell it biblically and by the way that I desire to live it out, prayer and worship seem to be synonymous in many ways. They are both communicational activities with refining and unifying qualities.

Perhaps one of the biggest differences can appear to be that worship sometimes comes with sacrifice. Throughout the scriptures we can see examples of worship in a variety of forms. Sometimes we see worship take place as a result of having come through some sort of hardship, and other times we see worship take place before the difficulty arises.

Prayer may not necessarily be associated with sacrifice in our minds, but it should certainly be connected to the trials that we face. Whether before or after hardships arise, prayer should be an ever present tool that we use to combat the lies of the enemy. Praying to the Conqueror of our adversary should bring about a great comfort and godly confidence when we need it most.

Prayer and worship in my own life are a dynamic duo. They create a buffer between my heart and mind, and they redirect the fiery arrows that relentlessly pursue me. The reason that they become that buffer is because they are faith-building investments.

If we invest our time in the presence of God, the benefits will flow into every area of our lives. When I spend time speaking with my Father in heaven, I am fixing my mind on eternal things, and when I sing of His qualities, I am proclaiming truths that overshadow any of the lies that try to take me down. Paul said in Ephesians 6:16, "above all, taking the shield of faith with which you will be able to quench all the fiery darts of the wicked one."

Faith rises in my heart when I spend time in the presence of the Lord. When His Spirit in me directs my life in a true lifestyle of prayer and worship, I know that my shield is up and constantly at work. It's in the times when I'm not investing in the truths of heaven that I feel those darts penetrating my heart.

When we pray and worship the Lord, we're communicating through eternally effective methods. They're about a relationship and not our performance. It's about a constant flow of dialogue, whether it's preventative or restorative.

A life of worship is more than a song; it's a walking relationship with the One who first loved us. He's worth living for because He gave His life to be with us.

CHAPTER THREE:

BE THE ONE

I've been married to my beautiful wife, Laura, for ten years now, and we have six children. My wife was born in England, and that is like a cool party trick or ice breaker at events. I can be a very socially awkward person at times, so this is the perfect conversation starter. To break the unpleasant silence, I love to pull the "Laura was born in England" card.

She moved out to America when she was four years old and has gone back and forth throughout her life. Last year, she had the opportunity to go back and visit her family, and she took our youngest son, Augustine, with her.

I took some vacation time to spend with our other four children while she was gone. I love being home with them; we have a lot of fun together. It also blesses my heart as a father because I feel like the more time I spend with them, the more I learn about their hearts, their gifts, and the ways that they desire to receive love. There are certain things about each of them at different times that pull on the strings of my heart.

Similar to my experiences with our kids, I believe that in the Bible we get the idea that there are things that touch the heart of our Father. I want to look at three stories of people in the New Testament who inspire me in the area of touching the heart of God.

One of those stories is found in John 13:23, when John wrote, "Now there was leaning on Jesus' bosom one of His disciples, whom Jesus loved." In the book of John, we read multiple times of the "disciple whom Jesus loved" and how he was always close to the heart of Christ.

Many believe that John was referring to himself when he wrote this. If that's the case, one could say that it was a bit pompous for him to write that title for himself. I tend to believe that it was not just by the allowance of God that it was written that way, but that it was by the divine inspiration of the Holy Spirit that John wrote it.

The reason I think this way is that I find great hope in the pursuit of being a disciple whom Jesus loves.

Now I don't say that to be prideful, nor do I believe somehow that I am going to be favored in any way above any of God's other children. However, I do believe there is a key to being the one that touches His heart, and I would say that it's intimacy, closeness, and a desire to stay near to Him.

If it was John sitting at the chest of Jesus, it's amazing to think that he was one of the few, if not the only person, to actually hear the physical heartbeat of God. It's not because Jesus wasn't accessible (He was available to all of His disciples), but there at that last supper there was only one disciple who seized the opportunity that no one else did. I wonder if he knew that in the next twenty-four hours that the heart that he was listening to would break for our sins. Do you think he knew that heart would stop beating? Or that on the third day it would start to pulsate again with resurrection power?

Maybe he did. Maybe the disciple whom Jesus loved had special insight because he spent the time to press in to Jesus.

We read that John was the only one of the twelve present during the crucifixion. Jesus told him that he was to be the new son of Mary. We also read that when Jesus had resurrected, John was the first one to the tomb...he even outran Peter! Finally, in John 21 we read that he was the first one to recognize Jesus when they were fishing.

There was a familiarity and zeal that we see in the "disciple whom Jesus loved." We don't necessarily find that same passion or pursuit in any of the other disciples.

John's life undoubtedly had trials. It was recorded that he was boiled alive in oil. It's not that his life was smooth sailing, but it's fascinating that God, in His infinite wisdom and sovereignty, allowed John to live the longest. He didn't pass away until somewhere about 100 A.D. Maybe it's because he exemplified the love of God so powerfully that the Lord used him all the way up until his earthly body was so weathered that it could not take anymore.

The example of John compels me to live a life that is in constant pursuit of intimacy with God through time in prayer, in His Word, and in worship.

Let me encourage you as a follower of Christ...use every moment as an opportunity to be in the presence of God. Yes, I do know that He's omnipresent. I know that God is everywhere all at once, but I also know that biblically there are manifestations of God's presence where He lingers with people as they approach Him expectantly.

I love the story in the second chapter of Acts. The disciples of Jesus were gathered in an upper room after the Lord had ascended back to heaven. They were waiting for a promise from the Father to be fulfilled.

Jesus said in Luke 24:49, "And now I will send the Holy Spirit, just as my Father promised. But stay here in the city until the Holy Spirit comes and fills you with power from heaven" (NLT).

We're told that there were about one hundred and twenty believers gathered in obedience awaiting the arrival of the Holy Spirit. When it happened at the time of Pentecost, the people who were all gathered were filled, and amazing miracles instantaneously began to take place.

The point is that sometimes we need to spend more time settling in to the presence of God, so that we don't rush into our daily tasks without the power that the Lord desires to impart to us for the completion of those very tasks.

Allow me to encourage you. God has not called you to settle for a disconnected relationship with your heavenly Father. Jesus' death made a way for us to approach the Father and Christ's resurrection ensured that by His Spirit we'd have access to God's presence because the obstacle of sin was shifted out of the way. Press in, press on, and press through.

Be the one.

CHAPTER FOUR:

APPROACH HIM AS FATHER

"Because you are sons, God has sent forth the Spirit of His Son into your hearts, crying out, 'Abba, Father!'" – Galatians 4:6

You see, we have a heavenly Father who loves His children so much. I think sometimes we underemphasize the title "Father" for our God. He's Savior, absolutely! He's Lord, yes! But He's also the perfect Father that none of us on earth have ever had.

It's very easy to forget the simple fact that if we are saved by grace through faith, the Creator of the universe, the God of all creation, and the Maker of the heavens and the earth, has adopted us as His children.

You might be sitting there thinking, *Well of course He's our Father. We talk about it, read about it, and sing about it often.*

That's all true, but I'd ask you this: how are you doing with simply being a son or daughter of the Most High? Are you currently walking in some overcomplicated version of a relationship with Him, or have you fully submitted yourself to the truth that you are a child of God, and that He is your Father?

Now, these statements might not be as heavy to us today as they may have been in past times. Take for instance a time before Christ when a veil that is believed to have been over three feet in thickness separated the holy of holies from the rest of the temple. The presence of God was so potent the high priest alone had access to it once a year.

Jesus changed that for us. We read in Hebrews 10:19-20, "And so, dear brothers and sisters, we can boldly enter heaven's Most Holy Place because of the blood of Jesus. By his death, Jesus opened a new and life-giving way through the curtain into the Most Holy Place" (NLT).

When Jesus died on the cross, the veil was torn in two, top to bottom our separation was annihilated to grant us uninhibited access to our Father.

I have found that in my flesh, I have a tendency to rebuild that veil with my own materials. Be it sin, shame, idols, a lack of time management, feelings of inadequacy, or any number of things. I rebuild something that Christ's sacrifice demolished for fellowship's sake.

Let us not forget the finished work of grace accomplished through Christ by the will of the Father, so that we can enjoy constant access into His presence.

Timothy Keller once said, "The only person who dares wake up a king at 3:00 a.m. for a glass of water is a child. We have that kind of access."

I love that picture so much. No one else has that kind of entry into a royal kingdom, let alone the King's bedroom. But we, as children of God, have been given the benefit of unobstructed access to the presence of the King (our Father) at all times.

DON'T REBUILD THE VEIL

Sometimes we unintentionally rebuild the veil, so to speak, by allowing the failure of man to create in us trust issues that build a wall between us and anyone else, including the Lord. I'd say that this is one of the most common reasons that people don't enjoy the benefits of being a child of God. It's not because He's not present, but it's because they are afraid to fully let Him in.

If you find yourself in that place, it's my prayer that throughout the duration of this book you will trust the fact that your heavenly Father is trustworthy and unfailing.

The words of the psalmist encourage me. "Your faithfulness endures to all generations; You established the earth, and it abides" (Psalm 119:90).

His faithfulness is eternally unshakable, but the ways of man are forever flawed. It's tragic to see so many people today take the name of our Lord in vain. They call themselves "Christians," some are even pastors, and they misrepresent the heart of the Father in the way that they treat others.

I've seen plenty of this throughout my life. I've seen people in authority abuse the platform that God gave them to take advantage of others. For a long time, I walked in trust issues because I was afraid of being hurt again. What the Lord began to show me is that if my trust is fully in man, then the degree of my hurt will be severe. However, if our trust is in the Lord, we might be hurt by man, but we will get through it because He will never fail us.

Fix your eyes on the goodness of God and open your heart to His desires for your life. His best for you is so much greater than what you can accomplish in your own strength. If you, like I was, are running in your own might, then you may be feeling tired, weary, and exceedingly guarded. Remember the truth that we find in Isaiah 40:31, "But those who wait on the Lord shall renew their strength; they shall mount up with wings like eagles, they shall run and not be weary, they shall walk and not faint."

They key is that we wait on the Lord, then He will exchange our perspectives of weakness for the eternal perspective of faith.

Approach your Father with a heart of willing surrender, and He will grant you the strength that you need.

CHAPTER FIVE:

THERE'S ALWAYS ROOM

I believe that it is very easy for us to reach a place of feeling as though we don't belong anywhere. It's one of the attacks of the enemy to make us feel excluded, maybe even like we are a burden to others. In extreme cases, the arrows of the devil will speak lies about how people would be better off without us.

That is a lie, but somehow we buy it.

One of the best things that we can do is combat those lies in faith through truths that we can cling to. One of those truths is that we always have a place to belong, and that's in the arms and comfort of our heavenly Father.

Like I said, I am a father of six beautiful children, and it's amazing the way that the Lord speaks to my heart through my interactions with my children. There's something lately that has been touching my heart in such a deep and profound way...they love to sit on daddy's lap.

If I go and sit on the ground anywhere near the area where they might be playing, it's only a matter of time until one of them comes over and plop onto my lap.

They could be in the middle of throwing a tantrum, or even just been hurt, yet they find such peace and contentment as they make their way onto my lap.

For some reason, my twin daughters, India and Scout, are the first of my children to do this on a regular basis, and it's frequent enough now that it has my heart in a deep meditation about the parallel that can be drawn to our heavenly Father.

India is the older of the two and her technique is generally that she'll walk right toward me, take one step onto my lap, gently twist her body around so that she is placed comfortably, and then she proceeds to nestle in.

Scout, the younger of the two, has a slightly more abrasive tactic. She runs toward me, dives onto my lap, and at some point will slip around until she's comfortable.

I can see in India's eyes as she's walking toward me that she is gentle and comfortable knowing that there is safety in the arms of her father. Scout will walk away from things that are holding her attention and will dive straight into a place where she will find affection and contentment.

Yesterday, I was compelled to call my four oldest children over to sit on my lap because I just wanted them to know that there is and will always be room for all of them on my lap, and more importantly, in my heart.

That got me thinking about where I run in times of trial as well as in times of victory.

If we're honest, I think that most of the time we run to a variety of things before we run to the arms of our Father.

In times of trial, some struggle with things like drinking more than they should, pornography, gossip, self-harm, social media, and much more. When we feel overwhelmed, we don't always know how to handle it or where to take it.

There is good news though! Our Father loves when we bring him our "overwhelmed" before we go anywhere else. He has strategically given us access into His presence to approach His throne of grace so that He can and should always be the first place that we turn.

I love with my children, any of the five that we have at home, that when they get hurt, they instinctively turn to their mother or father for comfort. We didn't have to teach our kids to do that. It's like they're in autopilot mode, with tears welling up in their eyes, their feet carry them to our presence and their arms are open the whole way over. They know the first place they should go when they are hurting.

That is probably true of most of us as children, but somewhere along the way something changed. The weight of life caught up with us and we became so serious all of the time. For some of us, now that we're older, turning to our

Father in heaven when we're hurt sounds like the tales of Neverland that we've forgotten since we've grown up. It sounds nice, but seems more fictitious than factual. Be encouraged though, if we can humble ourselves with willingness to run into the arms of the Father, it will never be in vain.

CHAPTER SIX:

NAMES MATTER

"Like arrows in the hand of a warrior, so are the children of one's youth. Happy is the man who has his quiver full of them; they shall not be ashamed, but shall speak with their enemies in the gate." – Psalm 127:4-5

It was Wednesday, May 12, 2010 and my wife was nine months pregnant with our first child. I had just made myself some curry for dinner because someone told us that it could induce labor. My wife had insane heartburn, so she couldn't eat the curry, but I thought I'd take one for the team.

As the night progressed, we were watching the ninth season of American Idol and my favorite contestant, "Big Mike," was being voted off the show. Right then, they began to hit. The contractions were three minutes apart from one another. We thought it might actually be the real thing, but there was also a sense of denial, being first time parents.

We called the hospital and they didn't seem all that concerned. They told my wife to take a shower and to see if the contractions were still close together afterward. We heeded the nurse's advice and Laura took a shower. The contractions continued to grow closer together, so we knew that it was time to take action. We arrived at Redlands Community Hospital at about 11:30 p.m. that night, and our son, Elijah James Enos, was born at 4:40 a.m. on May 13, 2010.

Little did I know that day how much our heavenly Father intended to teach me through parenthood.

Since then, my wife and I have had four more children. At the age of 26, I became a father to our fifth child, Augustine Jude Enos, on August 23, 2017. We have two sons, they are the bookends, and we have three girls in the middle. After Elijah we had our first beautiful daughter,

Harper Joy, on November 3, 2012. She brought so much joy to us in a season where we felt as though we were in a joy drought.

After we had one boy and one girl, we thought that we may have been done having children… obviously God had other plans! In 2015 my wife was pregnant for the third time, but something was different about this pregnancy. She became ill like I had never seen a pregnant woman become ill before. She was losing weight at an extreme rate and could not hold anything down, including water. This led to many trips to the hospital for IVs so that she could remain hydrated.

We found out when she was nine weeks pregnant that it was a "BOGO" pregnancy. She was pregnant with twins! On August 6th we met our beautiful identical twin daughters, India Bow and Scout Arrow.

The reason that I give you this backstory of how my wife and I became parents is because I think that it's so important to note that the God that we worship and serve with our lives is now a Father to us. Through being a father myself, I have had numerous epiphanies where I make connections with stories in the Bible and what I'm experiencing as I raise children of my own. Experiencing having a father's heart was the genesis of my revelation that our heavenly Father loves us so much more than we understand.

In this section of the book, I want to draw your attention to the fact that you are loved by your Father in heaven, the One who formed you physically, spiritually, and who has a plan and a purpose for your life. It's my prayer that as you understand to a greater degree how much God loves you, that it will invoke within you a greater desire for a lifestyle of worship.

You are loved and the more that you understand that, the more effective you will be in loving God and loving others.

YOU HAVE A NAME

As you may have noticed, some of my children have less-than-usual names. I promise you, each of their names has a purpose, and the purpose is not JUST to have kids with unique names.

If you are a parent, you understand that the names of your children are generally premeditated. I know for my wife and I, as we prayed through each of our children's names (while they were in the womb), we considered a couple things:

- What God was speaking in that season
- What we prayed for their future

For our firstborn, **Elijah James**, my wife and I had been going through the book of James. In chapter 5, James wrote about Elijah the prophet, who was a man like we are, but he had a great deal of faith when he prayed.

We knew going into having our first child that we needed a supernatural dose of faith, because we were young parents who had no idea what we were doing. The name Elijah came from our need as his parents. We needed faith, so we named our son according to our own need.

When we thought about Elijah growing up, we were praying that he would grow to be a man who would have unwavering faith when he prayed throughout his life.

Harper Joy came from a season when Laura and I felt like we lacked joy in our life. We were in a valley full of the "unknown" and it was unsettling at that time. In that season, worship was a tool that helped us through, so we knew that the Lord was speaking to us about worship and joy, so we wanted a name for her that spoke of those things.

When we prayed over Harper, as she would grow in stature and in the Lord, we knew that the Lord had a call on her life to be a worshiper and that He would use that in her life as a tool to produce joy when she felt like she lacked it. A harper is someone who plays a harp and in Psalm 43:4 the psalmist wrote, "Then I will go to the altar of God, to God my exceeding joy; and on the harp I will praise You, O God, my God." We prayed that verse would be something that she would carry with her name all of her life.

When we found out that we were having identical twin girls in 2015, we were overjoyed and nervous all at the same time. We were going from two children, a "normal" family size, to four children overnight!

At our first real appointment with my wife's doctor while she was pregnant with the girls, we received some really disheartening news. As the doctor was doing the ultrasound, he became oddly quiet. At the end of it he turned to my wife and said, "Your girls share an inner sac." Laura is a reader, so she already knew the risks that came with that. See, identical twins share one placenta, but they should have two separate inner sacs. This protects their individual amniotic fluid as well as each of their umbilical cords. When twins share an inner sac, there is a very high possibility that one, or both babies, will pass away from cord entanglement. That means that the cords could potentially tie together, which would cut off each baby's source of nutrition and oxygen.

That doctor is a Christian, so he asked if he could pray with us. I'll never forget in that prayer when he said, "Holy Spirit, will you create a barrier between these babies."

After that appointment, we had to wait for about a month until we went back for another visit. Those few weeks were some of the scariest that we've experienced as parents because we had no idea if our babies were alive or not.

When we went to our next checkup, I had to stay in the waiting room while my wife went back. It happened to be an anatomy scan, so it took close to an hour. In that time, I probably looked like a madman in the waiting room, pacing and praying out loud that the Lord would preserve the lives of our girls.

I remember praying a prayer that was inspired by Hannah, the mother of the prophet, Samuel. When she was barren, she cried out to the Lord begging for a son and promising that as soon as the baby was weaned, she would give him to the Lord to serve in His temple.

I prayed in that waiting room that if my heavenly Father saw fit to save these girls, that they would be His completely, His weapons of warfare.

After about an hour passed, my wife came out with joyful tears in her eyes, saying, "There are two sacs." God worked a miracle for our girls!

We named them *India Bow* and *Scout Arrow* because they are His weapons to use how He desires. India means "praise" or "give thanks" and Scout came from a prayer that they would be sent wherever the Lord desires to do His work.

When we found out that we were having our fifth child, another precious boy, we were incredibly grateful. We named him *Augustine Jude*. Augustine means "to increase" and Jude means "praise," so his name means "to increase praise." God was speaking to us at that time about how He is worthy of praise in every season. As we prayed about Augie and his life, we prayed that he would carry the praise of God everywhere that he would go in his life.

Then on Father's Day 2019, my wife and I found out that she was pregnant with our sixth child. I know that for many rational people that news would cause instant anxiety, but for me this was the greatest news we had received in quite some time!

From that day forward Laura was very sick. She has had varying degrees of morning sickness with each of our children, ranging from pretty bad to being in the ER consistently because she couldn't even hold down liquids. This pregnancy was not the worst, but it was up there for sure.

A few months into her pregnancy I went to England to lead worship for a festival, then a couple of weeks after I returned I went to Minnesota to lead worship for another event. During that time the Lord had been speaking to our hearts about how He is our refuge and our hiding place. I know that is a common theme in the Psalms and we talk about it often, but He was calling me to live it out in a greater way.

I was at LAX waiting to board a plane to Minneapolis when my wife and I settled on the name, **Cove Wilder**, for our sixth baby. We chose that name because it would be a constant reminder that we have a place of safety during the storms of this life…the Lord is our covering.

In that moment, we were in complete agreement that was to be our baby's name. The problem was that we didn't know the gender yet!

When I arrived in Minnesota, we decided to make an appointment to go to a 3D ultrasound place to find out the gender of our baby, so we made the appointment for the Friday after I returned.

The last night that I was in Minnesota, I was talking to my friends and they were sharing with me about the place where we were staying and how at one time it was called Restoration Cove. In that moment, the Lord confirmed yet again what our child's name was to be.

The Friday after I returned home, we woke up that morning with so much excitement. That was the day we would find out the gender of our baby! We loaded up our five kids and took them to the ultrasound place.

Once we were in the room, the tech started measuring the baby and taking photos. After a while she asked Laura to step out of the room and go to the restroom. While Laura was out there, the tech told her that she could not find a heartbeat for our baby. When she came back in the room, I looked into my wife's tear-filled eyes and instantly knew why she was distraught.

They confirmed that our baby was a boy, and that he had passed away a couple of days before the ultrasound. We had to wait a few days until we received the call that there was an opening at the hospital for Laura to go and deliver our baby boy.

We arrived at the hospital in the afternoon and at 2:58 a.m. our beautiful son was delivered. He was so tiny, yet so perfectly formed. We held him for hours, looking at his little hands and feet, weeping and in shock over the loss of our baby.

I never imagined that we would be called to live out Cove's name so quickly after the name was given to us. We were given a choice in the midst of the storm. We could run to the Lord with our pain, or we could run somewhere else where we would never find true healing. So we ran to the safest place we know—the presence of God.

In the middle of all of this, I had been texting my friend, Brian Eichelberger. He had helped my friend Emily and I write a song called, "Speak to Me" a few years before this. In the bridge of the song he had written the lyrics, "In the stillness You are with me, in the wild You are there." The day that we went to the hospital, Laura and I were both wearing shirts with those lyrics printed on them. We didn't plan that, it just happened.

I realized that the Lord had given us those lyrics to remind us that we would have calm moments in the "cove" of His presence, but there would also be "wilder" times that would come and He would be right there with us in those moments as well.

A couple days after we found out that our baby had passed away, my son Elijah said that he thought Wilder would be a good middle name for Cove. We would have never known how prophetic that name would be for us. Now, through the pain, we remember that we have a hiding place in the arms of our heavenly Father— the same place that our precious son resides.

Names matter.

A couple years ago, I had the opportunity to pray for a girl named Charity, and she was telling me about how she has a passion to be a nurse and to somehow use that in the mission field. The name Charity means "generous love" and when she was telling me about her passion to help people, all I could think was how amazing it was that the Lord gave her parents a name for her that would be prophetic to what she would want to be in life.

If we, being sinful human parents, have a desire to name our children something that carries promise, hope, truth, and value, how much more does our heavenly Father know us and name us according to His plan for us?

THE GIVER OF NEW NAMES

If we look at God's Word, we can see that names matter to the heart of our Father. This is why we see stories throughout scripture where God gave people a new name as He called them to something.

We see this first take place in Genesis 17:4-5, when God made a covenant with a man named Abram.

"This is my covenant with you: I will make you the father of a multitude of nations! What's more, I am changing your name. It will no longer be Abram. Instead, you will be called Abraham, for you will be the father of many nations" (NLT).

God changed Abram's name when He made him a promise. He told Abe that he would become a father of many nations. This was an especially odd promise, considering the fact that Abraham had no children with his wife Sarai, and they were both very advanced in years at the time. But God gave his wife a new name as well. It was Sarai, which means "princess," but God changed it to Sarah, which essentially means "someone married to a King."

God was calling this couple to something extraordinary, but not without affirming them by renaming them for the season ahead. In the same way, as we are brought from darkness to light, the Lord gives us a new name. He imputed His righteousness and made us co-heirs of the kingdom of God.

God told Abe and Sarah that they'd have a son and that his name would be Isaac. I love that the Lord told them the name well before the baby was in Sarah's womb. Let that be a reminder of God's love for you, even now. Before you were a thought in the mind of your parents (or an unplanned surprise), you were an intentional plan in the heart and mind of the Creator of the universe. He knew your name before anyone else knew you would exist.

I love the reminder that the Lord gave the prophet Jeremiah, "Before I formed you in the womb I knew you; before you were born I sanctified you; I ordained you a prophet to the nations" (Jeremiah 1:5).

That word from the Lord gave Jeremiah a confidence and dependency upon his heavenly Father throughout his life, and I pray that it does the same for you.

Abraham's grandson, Jacob, had an interesting life, particularly the time when he wrestled God and came out with a new name.

In Genesis 32:28 we read, "And He said, 'Your name shall no longer be called Jacob, but Israel; for you have struggled with God and with men, and have prevailed.'"

God gave Jacob the name Israel, and Israel had twelve sons which were the twelve tribes of Israel, and from them were born all of the "children of Israel." The nation of Israel is blessed because of the promise that God made Abraham...mind blown!

In the New Testament, Saul of Tarsus was a tyrant who abused and persecuted members of the early church. When Saul encountered Christ on the road to Damascus, everything began to change. Later we find out that Saul had a new name, Paul, which means "small." It would seem that the name Paul was indicative to the ministry of humility that lived for the remainder of his life.

Those are only a few examples from God's Word, but I hope that they serve as reminders of what your Father in heaven has spoken over your life.

Names matter to God because we matter to Him. He even gives us an extensive list of names, titles, and explanations of Himself from His Word. He didn't need to give us those. He knows His name and His power, but He loves us enough to give us truths about His character that help us understand Him better through each season.

He is "I AM," the God who spoke through a bush and granted deliverance to the Israelites. He is our Father, our Refuge, our Healer, our Inheritance, our Shepherd, our Potter, our Savior, our Friend, our King, our Creator, and so much more. Those are names and titles that we can cling to in times of need. Just as He has a name, He has given you a name and a calling.

Until you understand that you have a Father who called you from your mother's womb and gave you a name, you will not experience the zeal and passion for life that the Lord intends for you. Sometimes, in order to make a difference in the lives of others, we need to understand that God made us different. You have a unique name and purpose that the Lord has interwoven in the fiber of your being, so that you can walk in a God-breathed confidence in the fact that you are meaningful.

When the devil speaks in lies to make you feel ineffective, remember that you have a name in Christ. You are who He says you are. Cling to His promises and trust that He's not done with you. There is more to come. The best days can be ahead if you'll surrender to the plans and purposes that He's called you to.

CHAPTER SEVEN:

ONE FAMILY, MANY MEMBERS

"Yes, there are many parts, but only one body. The eye can never say to the hand, 'I don't need you.' The head can't say to the feet, 'I don't need you.' In fact, some parts of the body that seem weakest and least important are actually the most necessary. And the parts we regard as less honorable are those we clothe with the greatest care. So we carefully protect those parts that should not be seen, while the more honorable parts do not require this special care. So God has put the body together such that extra honor and care are given to those parts that have less dignity. This makes for harmony among the members, so that all the members care for each other. If one part suffers, all the parts suffer with it, and if one part is honored, all the parts are

[67]

glad. All of you together are Christ's body, and each of you is a part of it." – First Corinthians 12:20-27 (NLT)

It's a beautiful gift to look at my children, even at such a young age, and see such a diversity of gifts. I can see creativity through artistry and music, I can see compassion and discernment, I can see gentleness and boldness, I can see faith and humor. I see how each member of my family brings a much needed dynamic that would leave us lacking and incomplete if we didn't have them.

This is what Paul is telling us about the family of God in First Corinthians 12. We have been purposely formed and fashioned by our heavenly Father, to bring a piece that's missing to the body of Christ. You are not an accident. The way that your mind functions, and the unique gifts and abilities that you have been given, were intentionally woven into your being so that you can play a part in the body of Christ that no one else can perfectly mirror.

Think of your fingerprints—no one else shares them. They are completely and exclusively yours. Our twins are identical, which means that they share the same DNA. Indie and Scout look so similar that most people cannot distinguish between the two, yet they have one defining feature that sets them apart…they have unique fingerprints.

Now, this is very interesting, by sharing the same DNA, they could literally be framed for one another's crimes! I pray that this is a complete hypothetical and that there are never any crimes committed by those beautiful girls.

This is just to show that even with humans who are more similar than pretty much any other sets of people, they are still so unique. Aside from having their own fingerprints, they have their own personalities and specific callings from the Lord. I can see already how they have their own strengths and gifts.

Perhaps at this point in your life, you need to be reminded of how uniquely the Lord has created you. There's no one on earth who serves your unique purpose in the body of Christ. Before you were born, the Lord knew each of your days, every one of the hairs on your head, and the special call that He's placed upon you to walk in

His divine purpose and plan for your life. You are not an accident; you're a masterpiece.

Paul wrote in Ephesians 2:10, "For we are His workmanship, created in Christ Jesus for good works, which God prepared beforehand that we should walk in them."

The word "workmanship" in Greek is *poiēma* and it's where we get our English word "poem." I pray that transforms the way that you look at your life. You are God's special poem which He compiled for His glory.

On top of the fact that no one else serves the same purpose as you in the body of Christ, there's another amazing component of your individuality as a son or daughter of God…no one else can offer up your expression of worship.

We worship the Lord according to the way we see Him, and no one else sees Him the exact same way that you do. Every time you sing a song that refers to the goodness of God, or His faithfulness, prayerfully what's happening is that you're recalling specific seasons or answered prayers that remind you of how He has been good or faithful in your life.

When tragedy strikes and you desire to offer it up as an aroma of praise, no one else can offer it for you, and no one else can praise God from your exact experience.

When you feel like you're on a mountaintop, it's a great season to praise! When you're in a valley, it's still a great season to cry out in praise! Every season in between is an opportunity to spend time in the presence of God and allow His faithfulness to be the rock on which you're able to stand through every storm. You have the beautiful and unique opportunity to worship through the lens of your own life experience.

I'm reminded of this in the story of Noah. He built an ark when it made no sense. Noah was obedient in gathering all the animals and his family, loading them in the ark, and then spending a week in there before the rain began to fall.

It rained for forty days and forty nights, but the reality is that was only a small portion of the time that they would spend in that ark. In total it's believed that they were in that ark for just about an entire year!

Imagine spending a year in a boat with every type of animal. I can't even imagine spending a year on a boat with only humans, let alone humans and loads of smelly animals.

In Genesis 8:20-21 we read, "Then Noah built an altar to the Lord, and took of every clean animal and of every clean bird, and offered burnt offerings on the altar. And the Lord smelled a soothing aroma. Then the Lord said in His heart, 'I will never again curse the ground for man's sake, although the imagination of man's heart is evil from his youth; nor will I again destroy every living thing as I have done.'"

We see that what Noah decided to do after the storm was not complain, nor give in to hopelessness, but he decided to worship.

Now, this story is well before the Law was set in place requiring types of sacrifices. We get to see Noah's character as a worshiper of God. After the storm, but before the promise, he decided to offer a pleasing aroma to the Lord.

When we think of the rainbow and the promise to not destroy mankind again through a worldwide flood, we don't always think of it as being a result of worship, but it was.

The promise came after the praise, and often that can be true in our own lives as well. We have the blessing of worshiping the Lord because of the way that we see Him. It's possible that as Noah offered a sacrifice of praise to the Lord, he could have said something like, "You are the God who dries up the flood waters and preserves Your servants." You see, no one else before or after Noah's time would have been able to worship the Lord through that same lens.

Similarly, your life has been filled with ups and downs, joy and sorrow, healing and hurt, and no one else can see your heavenly Father exactly the way that you do. It's a gift, something that's a bond between you and your Maker, and no one can take it from you.

CHAPTER EIGHT:

YOUR GIFT IS YOUR KRYPTONITE

I've always been a fan of superheroes, ever since I was a child. I'd like to tell you that I've grown out of that phase of life, but I'd be lying. I still get every bit as excited about the newest hero movies as I did when I was younger.

Superman always seemed like such a superior hero compared to every other hero. He was not my favorite, but I always knew that he could ultimately defeat pretty much anyone or anything that came his way.

He did have one downfall though—kryptonite—that vibrant green alien mineral that glowed with a radiation that was crippling to Superman. It would make him weak and very sick when he was in its presence. Oddly enough, kryptonite was harmless to humans, so no one else would be affected by it, yet Superman would be on the verge of defeat.

I've come to learn that the gifts that the Lord has placed within each of us can also be an area of kryptonite when the enemy attacks us according to our gifts.

As a young child, I knew that God had called me to be a pastor when I grew up. In fact, when I was four years old, I walked out of my bedroom to tell my parents, "God just told me that I am going to be a pastor when I grow up." They were very loving followers of Christ, so they lovingly encouraged me to continue to pray about it throughout my life.

I was not given any specifics from the Lord. I didn't know whether I would be a youth pastor, a lead pastor, or anything else, but the word "pastor" was clear.

Around that same time, the attacks began. At the age of four, I was hurt by church leadership. I was in the middle of a big mess and at a very young age I got to see how flawed pastoral leadership can be.

Fast forward to my junior high years. My family and I attended a very large church and somehow I was again in the middle of a very bizarre situation. The pastor physically threatened me on multiple occasions. He had a very inappropriate relationship with a teenage girl whom I liked, and he had left bruises on my arms from grabbing and shaking me, then he told many lies about me.

This was a very pivotal time in my life. I was going through puberty, trying to discern the Lord's direction for my life, and I was hit with this major stumbling block as I watched a pastor instantly become the most toxic example in my life.

I began to ask the question: is this what it means to be a pastor? You hurt people and take advantage of them while abusing a God-given platform? It became a deterrent when it came to the pursuit of what God had called me to do.

I mean, what a perfect strategy, right? If the devil has been around since the inception of humanity, he has been observing the character, gifting, and callings of mankind. I believe that he tries to derail our life's calling as early as possible so that we cannot walk in all that God has destined us to do.

Thankfully, what the enemy intended for evil, the Lord used for good. One day, I had the opportunity to attend a midweek church service at a church called Calvary Chapel Pacific Hills. That evening, I heard the pastor teach through four chapters of John, and it ministered to me in a profound way, even as a 13-year-old boy. While he was teaching, I felt prompted by the Spirit to meet with him for counsel.

That week, I was able to meet with Pastor Dave Rolph for the first time. I shared my heart with him and he was able to graciously lead me in the right direction. I still praise God for that day as He divinely intervened in my life.

A few years later, I moved to Yucaipa, CA with my family. I was still damaged in my heart when it came to trusting church leadership. We had been invited to a church in town called Wildwood. I was very reluctant to try the church because ultimately I was afraid of being let down.

I'll spare you many details, but I eventually attended the youth group at Wildwood, and that night I met the senior pastor, Chris Fraley, and within a few weeks he took me to lunch and listened to my story.

That day I felt like someone saw value in what God had called me to in the area of music, art, and even pastoral ministry. Pastor Chris was willing to dream with sixteen-year-old me, and that was an invaluable gift to my life.

On December 15, 2013 one of God's promises was fulfilled in my life. I was ordained as a Pastor at Wildwood. Something that the devil worked relentlessly to hinder could not be stopped because it originated in the heart of my Father.

All this to say, you have gifts, God-given dreams and desires, and the devil has wasted no time attacking you in the area of your gifts.

I've begun to notice this pattern even with my children. My son, Elijah, is a natural born leader. He is confident, strong, and extremely talented. I can see that his strengths are also areas that he's most vulnerable to attacks. The devil wants Elijah's gift of leadership to be used for negative influence rather than leading people to the Lord.

I believe this is true of all of us.

Maybe you're naturally gifted at leading. Chances are that you're going to be attacked in the area of pride or anger.

Maybe you've got a compassion gift. I bet that the enemy has tried to dismantle your trust in people and caused you to be hurt one too many times, and so maybe you hurt people as a defense mechanism.

Maybe you've got a gift in discernment. The devil will try to get you to turn that gift into a critical spirit so that when God gives you an insight about someone, you write them off instead of praying and encouraging them in God's Word.

These are just a few examples, but I'm certain that if you survey your life, you will see that this has been true all along with the gifts that you've been given.

If you're a parent, I pray that this is an encouragement to you as it has been for me.

When you recognize the gifts in your children, it will help you be on guard to the attacks that will come their way.

Now, I believe that God has allowed for every trial in my life, and He has continued to work all things together for good in my life. At this point, I can say that I do not regret and I would not take back any of the things that happened to me in my youth, because I believe that I would not have the same confidence in what God has called me to if I didn't have those experiences.

If you've been hurt in your life and it has discouraged you from walking in what God has called you to, it's my prayer that you will allow for the love of God to dismantle the wall that's been built in your heart and that He will empower you to walk forward. He began a work in you, even when you were in your mother's womb, and He's faithful to complete it. Don't give up; give in to your Father's heart for your life.

CHAPTER NINE:
VANTAGE POINT

For some reason, it's very easy for us to be critical of others. When we got married, my wife, Laura, helped me realize how naturally a pharisaical attitude came to me.

I was a pro at pointing the finger at others, while I happily ignored the flaws that I continued to walk in. There were many denominations that I was very critical of, even to the point of not really fellowshipping with other Christians if they didn't believe the same things that I did.

Recently, I have a newfound joy when connecting with other followers of Christ from all around the world and different backgrounds. As I have been doing this, I've started to realize that many different churches hold fast to the Word of God, but they may emphasize different points.

For instance, there might be a denomination that has a very good grasp on the grace of God, and the result is that they trust in His sovereignty very well. There are others who emphasize the gifts of the Spirit of God, and the value of worship, because they understand the importance of intimacy with the Lord. There are others who practice a more liturgical style of church, and maybe they minister the value of order and how our God is a God who is into the details.

These are only a few examples, but my eyes have been opened to the fact that each of these are things that I need as I walk with Jesus. I read books from people that I disagree with, and prayerfully I can always walk away with something that will help me grow in my relationship with the Lord.

As long as it follows the Word of God, I believe that the body of Christ is made up of members who see God through a unique lens that becomes their vantage point. Just like a child sees a parent and knows them experientially, we can share about our heavenly Father based off our own experiences with Him.

I think this has the potential to change the way we view the global church. If we stop focusing on our differences and start acknowledging the strengths that we all have, then there is room for a unity within Christ's church like we haven't seen since the early church in Acts.

THE DYSFUNCTIONAL FAMILY

I'm pretty sure that none of us would choose (if we had the choice) to be a part of a dysfunctional family. Now, obviously to some degree, like it or not, there is some dysfunction in each of our families. No one is perfect. From my experiences, it would seem that people are generally trying to escape the drama in their families, they're not drawn to it for fun.

Jesus said, "By this all will know that you are My disciples, if you have love for one another" (John 13:35).

What if one of the biggest attacks on the church is to get us critical of one another and against each other so that to the world we appear as the dysfunctional body of Christ?

[85]

I really believe that people in the world are looking for love, and they're looking to be a part of something where they fit in. As they look in at modern Christianity, maybe the dysfunction becomes their deterrent. What if the unity of the church is meant to be one of our greatest tools for evangelism?

The world offers a faux "love" that affirms sinful lifestyles and strays from the truth of God. Maybe the people who are not Christians cling to the love that the world offers because they want a sense of belonging somewhere. If we're not loving each other the way that the Lord has commanded us to, we're missing out on the opportunity to show the world the true and greatest love they'll ever know.

This is by no means a blanket statement for the church as if it's failing. I think that in many ways the church is thriving and the Spirit of Christ is present and moving in many churches today.

I have just taken this on as a personal challenge lately, as a child of God, that I would be in the business of building bridges with other Bible-believing Christians, rather than burning bridges because they may see through a different lens than I do.

It's ok for me to read or listen to other pastors that I know I'll disagree with on some things. That doesn't mean that I go in with a microscope trying to pick it apart and find all the stuff I don't like. Instead, I go in looking for the thing that I need to hear. There's always something. For me, it's about honoring the work that the Lord is doing through that particular ministry, despite our differences.

Once the Lord opened my eyes to this, I began to realize how much I need others to share with me the way that they see our Father. In seasons of doubt, I read more of the people who trust His sovereignty. In seasons of spiritual drought, I read the ones who have a great handle on the practice of the presence of God. This helps me better understand the part that I play in edifying the body of Christ, and I hope it does the same for you.

CHAPTER TEN:
FAITH OF A CHILD

"About that time the disciples came to Jesus and asked, 'Who is greatest in the Kingdom of Heaven?' Jesus called a little child to him and put the child among them. Then he said, 'I tell you the truth, unless you turn from your sins and become like little children, you will never get into the Kingdom of Heaven. So anyone who becomes as humble as this little child is the greatest in the Kingdom of Heaven." – Matthew 18:1-4 (NLT)

A childlike faith gives us the ability to understand the kingdom of heaven in a way that we never can if we allow the cares of the world to become the majority shareholders of our attention.

We love to overcomplicate things. In an instant the most joyous of events can turn into an absolute burden because we start overthinking the simple joy that we're intended to experience.

As we enter adulthood, our faith can easily require more evidence than when we were children. Now, perhaps, instead of living out a constant dialogue with our Father through prayer and worship, we become increasingly more aware of the potential to look foolish, so we reel in our public display of adoration for our Redeemer.

I am so guilty of this.

"What will they think?" is the mantra of my flesh. It encourages me to find greater concern for the perception of man, rather than pleasing God. Although I can't remember a specific day that this began to change, I can trace it back to junior high.

I can look back to my seventh grade year and acknowledge the digression of my childlike faith. Prior to that there was such a simplicity about my relationship with God, the people of God, and leaders in church. I can see now the work of the enemy that allowed for my view of church leadership to be marred to a point beyond repair—or so I thought.

I had been mistreated, taken advantage of, and my simple childlike faith changed into something that required constant proof of validity because I had trust issues in the faith department.

Here I am years later finding such value in spiritual growth: being a student of the Word, walking in worship, studying theological material, and so much more. But for me, these things must begin with the simple understanding that God, my Father, values my heart of simple faith more than He desires the things that I can do for Him.

Our "works" should always be the overflow of a loving relationship. They should bring us joy because we get to do them for the One we love, not because we have to.

If you, like I have before, find yourself going through the motions of Christianity, rather than living out the daily adventure of faith, I encourage you to return to a simplicity of heart. Love God, love His people, and serve from the overflow of that love. Have faith like a child and watch your Father restore your sense of spiritual adventure.

I WONDER

To me, one of the keys to having childlike faith is not losing the wonder of who God is and who He says I am. Sometimes, it's good for me to get lost in the grandeur of creation.

Paul wrote in Romans 1:20, "For since the creation of the world His invisible attributes are clearly seen, being understood by the things that are made, even His eternal power and Godhead, so that they are without excuse."

What Paul is saying there is that God has attributes that are invisible, but can be perceived as we look at the things that He's made.

When I look at you, I see an invisible characteristic of God embodied. When I look at the sky, I see something so grand and overwhelming that it could only have come from God. When I look at my wife, my children, my family, and my friends, I see a community that's only possible because of the unity that God has created for the purpose of eternal fellowship.

Don't ever stop taking the opportunity to smell the roses. Don't ever stop making time to pull over and just lose your breath at the sight of the mountains or the sea.

Don't ever lose the wonder.

PART THREE:

YOU HAVE A FATHER

UNDERSTANDING THE PRIVILEGE THAT YOU'VE
BEEN GIVEN TO CALL GOD, FATHER

CHAPTER ELEVEN:

MY DAD IS THE STRONGEST

I can remember as a child living with constant belief in my father's strength. I genuinely thought that he was invincible.

There was one time that my dad and I drove home and when we got there he realized that we were locked out of the house. He went around and checked all of the doors before desperation led to the unthinkable. At four years old, I watched my dad punch through a window to break it so we could enter the house!

It cut up his hand a little bit, so there was some blood. For some reason, in my mind, that meant that his death was imminent.

I screamed and cried, "I don't want you to die!" I can remember the look on his face. He was getting frustrated as he wiped the blood from his hand because he knew that the wounds were minor, yet my reaction was not.

The point is this, that day I realized that my earthly father, my hero, was not invincible, but that didn't stop me from believing that he could beat up anyone else's dad if he so desired!

Now, as a father myself, I can sometimes see a similar perspective in the eyes of my children. They look at me like I am heroic, as if I can accomplish anything I desire. As much as I appreciate my children's belief in my abilities, I know my limitations. If they only knew how incapable I am of the things they think I am able to do!

As children of God, we can never overestimate His power and strength. Paul reminds us in Ephesians 3:20, "Now all glory to God, who is able, through his mighty power at work within us, to accomplish infinitely more than we might ask or think" (NLT).

There's not even a way to measure how much greater He is than we know. We all have dreams that seem out there and unattainable; yet, even then His plans for us are immeasurably greater and more effective. If He has planted a God-size dream in your heart, please trust that He is big enough to water it until the day that it bears the fruit that your heart dreams of.

When we live like "my Father is stronger than yours," we couldn't be more spot-on! Our Father is the Maker of the heavens and the earth. Our Father is the One who created the angels, including one that went rogue named Lucifer.

Think about it, the one pulling the strings of all the evil in the world is a fallen angel, a created being. He is the ruler of the darkness of this age, and sometimes we live in crippling fear because of the effects of his reign. We know that there is a hierarchy of angels, so it's possible that Lucifer was a high ranking angel, but even at the top, they are still infinitely inferior to the God that created them.

What am I getting at here? Don't ever forget whose Spirit lives in you. You are a child of God. The God that created all things, the God who cannot be boxed in, or fully understood by any creation.

A GIVING FATHER

"If a son asks for bread from any father among you, will he give him a stone? Or if he asks for a fish, will he give him a serpent instead of a fish? Or if he asks for an egg, will he offer him a scorpion? If you then, being evil, know how to give good gifts to your children, how much more will your heavenly Father give the Holy Spirit to those who ask Him!" (Luke 11:11-13).

James, the brother of Jesus, said it well in James 1:17. "Every good gift and every perfect gift is from above, and comes down from the Father of lights."

What if we as the body of Christ, as the bride of Christ, as servants of God, and as people of God, made a conscious effort to expectantly approach our Father, trusting that He is the giver of every good and perfect gift?

Sons and daughters of the Most High, your benefit as a child of God, filled with the Spirit of God, is that you have the ability and responsibility to draw near to your Father at all times. Whether in times of hardship or smooth sailing, He desires to be closer than the air that we breathe.

So we have a choice today. Will we make our way to Daddy's lap where there is room for any and all of His children, or will we try to make it in our own effort?

Remember that every good gift comes from Him to those who seek after them.

When we are in the valley, when we are on a mountaintop, or anywhere in-between, we are faced with a decision...approach Him as Lord and Savior, or as Father. We are children of God and that comes with benefits.

When was the last time that you spoke to God as though He is your Father who wants to give you good gifts? Is there regularity to your relationship with Him, or is He like a lifeline on *Who Wants to Be a Millionaire* that you only use when you're stuck and afraid to lose it all?

CHAPTER TWELVE:
EYE CONTACT

I have this fascination with the story of Peter walking on water. I love the audacious faith that it took to step out onto the water. What it must have been like to abandon his knowledge of nature and step out into the wonderful miraculous, with Jesus as the Lord bending the laws of nature to demonstrate His power.

We can see through reading the story that at some point Peter began to look at the power of the storm more than he acknowledged the power of the Lord, and that's when he began to sink.

I feel like up until that moment, Peter was locking eyes with the Son of God, then suddenly he was completely aware of the dangers and impossibilities that he was standing upon.

At some point, something caught Peter's eye, and it wasn't Jesus' eyes. It was the eye of the storm, it was the epicenter of the chaos, and the firmness of the water subsided with his faith in that moment.

I love sinking Pete's response. He exclaimed, "Lord, save me!" See, although we can look down on Peter for his lapse of faith, we can applaud him for knowing where to turn when he began to sink. He asked for the help of the Lord.

One absolute key element of this story to me is eye contact. I guess I feel like if Peter's eye contact with Jesus would have been uninterrupted, Peter may have not fully sunk. Of course, it's speculation to some degree, but I feel like it's a fair one.

I love being a father. It's one of my greatest joys in life, along with being a husband to my wife. It makes my heart leap out of my chest when I am getting ready to walk in the door to my house after a long day of work, and I can hear my two oldest children behind the door chatting about how they can hear me and I'm finally home.

When I finally get the door open, they rush into my arms and talk a million miles a minute. Then I look into the living room and immediately my eyes are greeted by one of my two twins, Augie, Harper, or Elijah, and inevitably the first one to lock eyes with me gets the first kiss.

Now, this is not something that I've planned out, this is not some form of punishment to the other children for not looking first, but it's my paternal instinct as a loving father to approach the child who was anticipating me first.

I wonder if it's the same way for our heavenly Father. I wonder if eye contact with heaven is key to the way that He approaches us. Is expectancy to encounter Him a way to play the strings of His heart, so to speak?

Is it a fair assumption to say that when you walk into church expectant, that the Lord is drawn to you in a special way? Maybe not, but I can only speak as a father created in the image of God, and I think that it's a genuine possibility.

We should purpose in our hearts to not break eye contact with our Father. Remember, like Peter walking on water, He is always the one who holds the power for us to accomplish the impossible. At our best, we're still just the ones who are trusting our God with undivided attention.

CHAPTER THIRTEEN:
NO FEAR IN LOVE

I recently went to the beach with my family. Now, an unimportant detail of this book is that there is something in me that loathes the ocean. Deep down inside it's probably my greatest fear.

It's full of creatures unknown to me. Its depths are unknown to me. There seems to be a great deal of unpredictability when it comes to the ocean, and I don't like it.

The horizon is absolutely beautiful to look at, but my overly analytical brain looks out with anxiety of the unknown.

Well, it's obvious that I grew up with a chip on my shoulder when it comes to the beach. I was never allowed to go in very deep as a child, which meant I stayed on the sand a lot, and I'm not too fond of the sand either.

But this time when I went to the beach with my family, I decided to press through my own fears for the sake of their enjoyment. I really wanted my children to have fun.

My daughters, India and Scout, were terrified of the water. When my wife walked with them in the water, they cried and began to shake out of fear.

About an hour later, I picked Indie up and went out into the shallow breaks of the waves. As I held her and made a game out of bringing her into the spray of the water and quickly lifting her out, she began to giggle and eventually was busting up in laughter.

I repeated the same thing with Scout (who was the more reluctant of the two that day) and she displayed the same joyous reaction.

All of the insecurities that those girls had about the ocean were overshadowed by their confidence in their me.

In the same way for us, we encounter situations in life that we are unsure of and fearful to approach, but entering them alone, or holding the hand of our Father, will make all of the difference in the world.

See, our heavenly Father is not just a title given for us so that we can have an endearing name to use in prayer. It was not just given so that we could worship Him in a religious way and sound closer to Him because we call Him, "Father."

I believe that the Lord has given us the ability to be called children of God so that we can walk in a godly assurance that we're never alone and that we have access to our heavenly Father just like a child should have access to their father.

We have the ability to walk hand-in-hand with our Father through every trial, tragedy, or triumph. He's not going anywhere. He desires closeness in everything, but we must say "yes" to His heart.

I've really been enjoying hiking in the local hills here in Yucaipa, CA. It's beautiful to look out and see such a magnificent landscape surrounding us where we live.

One day, I had this epiphany. I thought, *I am looking out and enjoying my Father's creation, so why don't I go out into that creation to enjoy Him?* So I began going for little hikes up into the hills and praying for the city as I did so.

Before I had gone to the top of the highest hill near me, I decided that it would be a good idea to take my son, Elijah, (who was seven years old at the time) and Harper (who was four years old) to the top with me.

By the time we got about 3/4 of the way up, I realized that it was probably not a good idea to take my kids up with me before I had gone up myself. So I consistently asked them if they wanted to turn back, and their mutual consensus was that they wanted to reach the top.

Since I had not gone up before, I didn't know that there were multiple ways to the top, and we just happened to stumble across the one that gets unreasonably steep right before the top.

As we approached what looked like a dirt wall, which at that point appeared to be the only way up, we proceeded with reluctance.

Harper began to get tired and asked if I would hold her as we went up, so I lifted her in my arms and continued on.

Then I told my son to give me his hand. He wanted to be brave on his own, but I insisted that he held my hand. He asked one more time if he could let go, and right as he uttered those words, he lost his footing and didn't fall down that steep portion of the hill because he had my hand in his.

That was the last time he asked to let go. He held my hand with joy after he realized the possibility of falling!

I feel the same way in my relationship with our Father. I find myself at times asking if I can do it on my own, and right then He saves me from falling.

Other times, I don't even ask, I just let go. When we fully let go of His hand, sometimes we experience a fall that will jolt us and instill a healthy fear.

His righteous and mighty hand is always with us to hold us, to catch us, to lift us, and to fight off adversaries. All we have to do is hold on and trust. Don't let go. We're never in a better place after we release the hand of God.

HE DOESN'T LET GO

One of my friends who is a father gave me some great advice recently. All of his kids are adults now, and this man is filled with the genuine love of Jesus. What he told me pricked my heart in a holy fashion. He said, "Whenever you hug your kids, never be the first to let go."

He proceeded to share with me about how that is one of the best ways to show our children that we will never stop loving them. When we not only make ourselves available to them, but also hold on until they let go of us, we're exemplifying the love of our Father to our children.

This is the way that God loves His children—He never lets go. He holds us even when it hurts Him. We can choose to walk away from our Father for a season, but He's waiting with open arms for our return.

In Luke's Gospel, Jesus was sharing a parable about a son who was living a prodigal lifestyle. He wasted all that he had, and when he had nothing left, he found himself hanging out with pigs and desiring their food because he had none for himself.

Once the prodigal recognized his mistake, he made his way home. Jesus said in Luke 15:20, "And he arose and came to his father. But when he was still a great way off, his father saw him and had compassion, and ran and fell on his neck and kissed him."

That is our heavenly Father. When we're serving and loving Him well, He holds on. When we're prodigal, His love holds on. When we make our way home, His open arms receive us and He holds on.

In fear and faith, He holds on.

He doesn't let go.

CHAPTER FOURTEEN:
THE FAMILY BUSINESS

Throughout the ages, sons have inherited family businesses. In fact, Jesus was a carpenter by trade like his earthly father, Joseph. Traditionally, fathers would raise up their sons to learn the family business from a young age. The sons would observe their fathers' work ethic, techniques, and they would probably marvel at how awesome they thought their dads were.

Jesus was a carpenter, but He had a greater purpose upon His life. In Luke chapter 2, Mary and Joseph realize that as they had been traveling back home from Jerusalem after the Passover feast, Jesus was not with them. He was only twelve years old and they went three days without knowing where He was. They were anxious and frantically looking for Him, so they traced their steps back to Jerusalem. As they were searching, they went into the temple and, to their surprise, found Jesus sitting in the midst of the teachers, listening and asking them questions. When they asked him why He stayed behind, He said, "Why did you seek Me? Did you not know that I must be about My Father's business?" (Luke 2:49).

Jesus had a job here on earth. Isaiah prophesied about it in Isaiah 61:1, saying, "The Spirit of the Lord God is upon Me, because the Lord has anointed Me to preach good tidings to the poor; He has sent Me to heal the brokenhearted, to proclaim liberty to the captives, and the opening of the prison to those who are bound."

Jesus accomplished those things because He was "about [His] Father's business." Jesus also said, in John 5:19, "I tell you the truth, the Son can do nothing by himself. He does only what he sees the Father doing. Whatever the Father does, the Son also does" (NLT).

The relationship between the Father and Son of the Godhead should be our greatest inspiration for our spiritual work ethic.

Just as Jesus had a job to accomplish here on earth, we do as well. Jesus gave us some instructions before He ascended to heaven after the resurrection. In Matthew 28:19-20, He said, "Therefore, go and make disciples of all the nations, baptizing them in the name of the Father and the Son and the Holy Spirit. Teach these new disciples to obey all the commands I have given you. And be sure of this: I am with you always, even to the end of the age" (NLT).

Jesus told us to go and make disciples of all the nations, and the only way to do that is by proclaiming the Gospel and being examples of His love. Jesus said in John 13:34-35, "So now I am giving you a new commandment: Love each other. Just as I have loved you, you should love each other. Your love for one another will prove to the world that you are my disciples" (NLT).

Jesus asked us to observe the way that He exemplified love, and to practice and walk in that same love so that the world would look at the church and see a love that didn't look like anything that the world could offer.

Love is always the bridge by which the truth should be conveyed. That's the example that

Jesus lived out before us. His love was the evidence to people that He was trustworthy. To a woman caught in the act of adultery, Jesus would tell the gang about to stone her that the person without sin could cast the first stone. Since Jesus was the only one without sin, He chose not to cast a stone, but to build a bridge in love. He asked the woman, "Where are your accusers?" She said that they were gone, and He said, "Neither do I [accuse you]. Go and sin no more."

Before Jesus told her to stop living in sin, He showed her His benevolent heart of love.

LIVING WATER

Another story that I love about Jesus building a bridge to convey truth is found in John chapter 4. Jesus stopped at a well in Samaria (which the Jews would have never done at that time), and He met a woman there and asked her for a drink.

Right off the bat, the woman was caught off guard that a Jewish man would be speaking to a Samaritan woman.

Jesus told her, "If you knew the gift of God, and who it is who says to you, 'Give Me a drink,' you would have asked Him, and He would have given you living water."

After they had a great conversation about worship, Jesus asked about her husband. She told Him that she wasn't married. Jesus appreciated her honesty and told her that He knew she had been married five times before, and now had a relationship with a man who was not her husband.

Jesus offered the woman living water before he pointed out her sinful lifestyle. Unfortunately, this is something that we get backward sometimes.

It's really easy for us to point out other people's sin before we offer them hope, but that's just not the way that Jesus ministered to the world. We are called to preach the Gospel of hope to the world, and to be examples of love.

GOOD NEWS

There's a lie from the devil floating around that because some are offended by the Gospel, that the church needs to shy away from talking about sin.

The fact is that if we don't talk about sin, we don't understand grace. You can't sing out "Amazing grace" without understanding that it "saved a wretch like me."

There's a movement of people that don't want to mention the blood of Jesus because it might offend. I don't know about you, but the understanding that it was either His blood or mine, makes it an incredible gift of love.

"What can wash away my sin? Nothing but the blood of Jesus. What can make me whole again? Nothing but the blood of Jesus." The blood of Christ is a precious gift that acts as a centerpiece to our salvation.

There is no sacrifice that we could ever offer that would have completely covered our sin. You see, we are all conduits by which actions flow. Be it actions flowing from a source of sin, or actions flowing from the source of His Spirit and grace. Things flow out of us: our words, our behaviors, maybe even our facial expressions.

Being a conduit comes from Yahweh because from Him flows every good and perfect gift, from Him flows love incomprehensible, and from the Son flowed blood that contained a purity with the power to purify and rid humanity of sin if they'd receive it. This is good news!

God's Word tells us in a parable that it's like there's a big heaven party and He invited family (Jews) first, but because they were too busy the invitations went out to everybody.

That's why in Romans 1:16, Paul said, "I am not ashamed of the gospel of Christ, for it is the power of God to salvation for everyone who believes, for the Jew first and also for the Greek." Aren't you grateful that we received the invitation to that heaven party where Jesus and His bride are the central theme? I sure am!

I believe now more than ever that a life of worship is a life that walks in awe of the Gospel. If we allow ourselves to become ashamed to echo the truth of the good news about Christ, then we are in a sense forfeiting our influence for the furtherance of the Gospel. Jesus said, "Nor do they light a lamp and put it under a basket, but on a lampstand, and it gives light to all who are in the house. Let your light so shine before men, that they may see your good works and glorify your Father in heaven" (Matthew 5:15-16).

The light that we have to illuminate should be a noticeable difference because of the Spirit of God that has been imparted to us, thanks to the Gospel. This is why we should walk with the truth on our lips so that we can influence the culture around us with hope that's only possible through Christ.

RIGHT IN FRONT OF YOU

"Do not despise these small beginnings..." – Zechariah 4:10 (NLT)

Often it's easy for us to try to shoot for the stars in terms of who we'll minister to. For those who serve in the area of worship, sometimes we think that we're ineffective unless we're writing songs with the top songwriters or leading at the biggest conferences. For those who serve with their teaching gift, we can believe the lie that we don't matter if we're not preaching at a megachurch or have our own podcast.

We need to make sure that we measure success according to quality and not quantity.

If there are only a few in front of you, serve them wholeheartedly. If there are many, don't lose sight of the faithful servants that work unseen. Every sheep in the fold of God matters to Him dearly, and they should to us as well. They are not placed in some value system according to the perception of their importance. Jesus is not into partiality. His ministry exemplifies that for us in such a profound way.

Christ spent His time with despised and unqualified people. He exalted the faith of the sick and multiplied blessings for the poor.

Jesus poured Himself out in discipleship for twelve men. Jesus was and is able to disciple the entire world in an effortless fashion if that's what He wanted to do, but instead He gave us an example of faithfulness.

Whatever or whoever God has put in front of you, be careful that you do not look at them as a stepping stone, but rather an opportunity to show the heart and love of your Father. Remember that He sees your heart. We can't fool the One who made us. He knows when you serve out of the wrong intentions, and He knows exactly how far He'll let you go before He corrects that in you.

Serve with joy, wherever God has you, and He will bring the increase according to your faithful heart to love Him and His people.

CHAPTER FIFTEEN:
TO THE FATHERLESS

Maybe you've read up to this point and deep down you feel like you cannot fully relate because your relationship with your father was not the way that it should have been, or maybe you don't have a father.

Perhaps it's difficult for you to accept the love of your heavenly Father because all you know of a father figure is some form of abuse and letdown. Please do not disregard the principles from this book because someone has been a poor example of love to you. The misrepresentation of love in your life is not the heart of your heavenly Father.

If you've been mistreated by a father figure, it's with the utmost sincerity as a father that I say I'm so sorry.

Since the fall of man in Genesis, we've been living in a world that operates in the context of sin, and some people continually give in to their depraved nature rather than allowing Christ to dwell in them and to change their hearts. If you had a bad father, it's not because God wanted them to mistreat you. It's because they were walking in sin and not in God's best for them.

The beautiful thing about our Father is that He gives us the opportunity to start a new pattern of living as He breaks the former chains that bound us. What I mean is this—if you have the Spirit of Christ living in you, and you had horrible parents, then you have the opportunity to be the kind of parent that you wish you had growing up.

If you come from generations of drunkenness, abuse, perversion, gossip, or any other sinful pattern, then you have the ability in Christ to break that pattern and start a new pattern of parenting with the love of Christ.

It's important to note that this is only possible through His strength. You cannot do it in your own power, but you can do all things through Christ who strengthens you.

Maybe you never knew your father because he was absent at your birth. Your heavenly Father has never and will never abandon you. It's inexcusable that anyone would walk away from the priceless gift that you are. I pray that you find rest and assurance in the fact that the Lord will never walk away from you. He will only ever run toward you with open arms.

THE PAIN OF LOSS

Maybe you lost your earthly father and you're confronted with the immense grief and pain that comes from that loss. I am so sorry that you have experienced that type of deep pain.

I want to reiterate to you that death was not intended for mankind. In man's "garden state," we were made in the image of God and built for eternity with Him. When sin entered the picture, death crept in with it. It's a direct result of the disobedience of man, not a product of the heart of the Father.

Just like I wrote earlier, one of the shortest verses in the Bible tells us that Jesus wept. A part of me wonders if He was weeping because of the loss, the pain, the doubt—all these were things that man was not intended to feel in Eden.

If you're experiencing any of those things, I pray that you find some comfort in the words, "Jesus wept." God's heart breaks for the broken. He's with you in the pain, and no matter what other people will tell you, He is the only One who will ever know how you feel.

People try their best to offer encouragement in moments of loss, and one of the most common is, "I know exactly how you feel." As well intentioned as they are, this is simply not true. There can be two people who experience the exact same situation, and they still would not know the way the other one feels. This is because we're all built differently. Like we talked about previously, we all have different gifts, filters, strengths, and weaknesses.

I pray for you that you embrace the closeness of your heavenly Father. In the pain, sorrow, loss, and frustration, He's not offended by your emotions. He desires that you bring all of them to Him so that He can show you why He's called the "God of all comfort." He wants to show you a peace that passes your understanding.

I believe that the more you allow your heart to nestle into the love of God, the more that you'll find the healing you desire. The healing is only in part, because full healing only comes when we're in heaven. Still, I know that He'll give you the daily dose of healing that you need, just like manna from heaven, so that you can make it through each day by His grace.

What the enemy intends for evil, the Lord will use for good in your life—even the pain of loss. In our hands, loss only means that we're left without, but in God's economy, loss is an opportunity for Him to fill us in miraculous ways.

From the heart of a father and friend, please know that I do not believe that God is the source of your pain, but that He will be the source of your healing.

When I look at my children, I see precious gifts that I would never intentionally hurt just so they can learn a lesson. For instance, when I look at the fire, I tell them, "Don't touch the fire." If they touch the fire, I kiss their finger, I say a prayer for them, and I cuddle them. What kind of dad would I be if I stuck their finger in the fire and said, "That hurts, doesn't it? Don't do this again." That wouldn't seem very loving, right?

It implies something similarly strange when we say that God caused our loss and that it was somehow to teach us a lesson. That doesn't make us feel very loved. Instead, that kind of wrong thinking makes us feel really confused.

God is sovereign; He knows beginning to end. There is no trial that will come our way that He does not allow, but I don't believe that He's some puppeteer who is using evil circumstances to teach us a lesson. Since He's referred to as Father, all I have is the Word of God and my experience as a father to lead me to the conclusion that He works from a heart of love and that He's not tormenting us to prove a point.

Paul wrote in Romans 8:28-29, "And we know that all things work together for good to those who love God, to those who are the called according to His purpose. For whom He foreknew, He also predestined to be conformed to the image of His Son, that He might be the firstborn among many brethren."

Nothing in your life is wasted. In your pain, He is conforming you to the image of His Son. That means that you will know an element of the heart of God that some others may not. In your heartache, draw near to your heavenly Father and He will draw near to you every time.

PART FOUR:

CONCLUSION

UNDERSTANDING HOW TO MOVE FORWARD IN
YOUR RELATIONSHIP WITH YOUR FATHER

CHAPTER SIXTEEN:
ELEMENTAL APPLICATION

I'm so blessed that you've made it this far in our journey to the simplicity of a walk with God. I realize that this book is a formulation of many different topics and themes, so you may be wondering how you can practically apply some of these themes to your life.

When thinking through the conclusion of this book, what is on my heart is to reiterate the importance of some of the things that we practice regularly as Christians, but with maybe a new simplicity that will reinvigorate a passion for these simple practices.

Let's look at four things that will keep our relationship with God both relational and healthy. Now, these are not in any particular order of importance, but they are listed in the order of how they appear daily in my life.

PRAYER

Paul wrote in First Thessalonians 5:17, "Never stop praying" (NLT). The only way that's possible for me is if I allow for God to transform the way that I look at prayer. If I only see prayer as a time when I'm on my knees crying out to God, then I practically have to stop that at some point because I'd inevitably need to use the restroom and eventually eat (I get hangry and delusional if I let too much time pass between meals). I don't think God wants to hear anything from me in that state of mind, but that's beside the point.

In order to follow this command to remain in a perpetual state of prayer, I have to view prayer as an ongoing conversation with my Dad. I know this may seem strange, but first thing in the morning, maybe before you even open your eyes, the conversation should begin. "Thank You, Father, for this new day. Lead me in all that You desire for this day." It can start briefly and simply, but He should be the first place we turn with our thoughts, with our hearts, and with our actions.

Moment by moment, the conversation should continue. If you're frustrated on the freeway, talk to Him about it. If you receive good news, talk to Him about it. If you receive bad news, talk to Him about it. Talk to Him like He's real, because He is.

Some of my favorite times with my heavenly Father are spent walking and talking. Sometimes it's audible (and I look crazy), while other times it's in my heart. There is something so special about experiencing His presence while spending time in nature. When looking out at the mountains, the trees, the birds, the sky, and the people all around, it reminds my heart that God, our Father, is so much bigger than the things I struggle with, and He's far more grand than we are.

Pray with the simplicity of a child, with the authority of the Spirit that raised Jesus from the dead, with faith that can move mountains, and everything in between. Talk to God. Get into the habit of doing it more and more. Fall in love with the access that you have to seek Him with every breath. It's real. It works. Never stop praying.

READ THE BIBLE

This is a fun one for me, but it wasn't always. If I can be honest with you (which we're friends now, so I think I can be), I feel so inferior to those people who know every verse in the Bible. I say that only partially exaggeratedly. There are some people who know the Bible *so well*. They know every book, what's happening in every chapter, and they know the verse references. Unfortunately, I don't naturally have one of those minds that can memorize things easily.

My feelings of being inferior honestly held me back from really digging into the Word of God for a long time. I felt like if I read the whole Bible, I just wouldn't understand everything, and then it made me scared to even try.

Everything changed when I realized that the Bible was just another opportunity for my heavenly Father to reveal Himself and spend time with me. I finally began to understand that biblical knowledge was not a hoop that I had to

[138]

jump through to earn His favor, but it is actually just one of the ways that He speaks His heart for us. It's not about knowing the chapters and verses—those are just tools to help us—they actually weren't even there on the original scrolls!

The point of spending time in God's Word is that we gain a better understanding of who He is and how He loves us.

My grandpa was in the Navy during WWII, and he and my grandma had such an amazing love story. One of my life goals is to write a book about them...you guys can keep me accountable in that.

I used to love sitting with Grandpa to hear the stories straight from his mouth about how he met Grandma in New York City, and how they fell in love. He came home just for a day before being deployed again, so they quickly ran off to New Jersey to get married, and then he left the next day.

They would correspond with handwritten letters (apparently they didn't text back then). He would tell me about how they had special codes so that she'd know where he was headed since he couldn't tell her by name. Before my grandpa passed away, I received one of the greatest treasures of my life…the box of letters they sent to each other.

I absolutely loved hearing the stories from Grandpa as he'd share. Every so often, I'll look at that box of letters, and I'm amazed at the fact that I get to hold a piece of history that brings me into the narrative of their love story.

Allow the Word of God to be the same for you. Don't read it because you think it will make you a better Christian, read it because God has a message that He wants to share with you. He has a story that included you before you ever knew it.

If we allow for His Word to become a textbook so that we just grow in knowledge, then it's very easy for us to end up with a pride that's reminiscent of the Pharisees. However, when we read it relationally, we'll end up with a wisdom that's reminiscent of the psalmists.

I hold fast to the cliché about Christianity being a relationship, not a religion. The reason why is because when I look at my time with God as being an obligation, I miss out on the joy of spending Father-son time and turn it into something that I don't believe the Lord wants for me.

When you think outside of the box about the way you read the Bible, it takes on new power in your life. Open up the Gospels and don't put pressure on yourself to read five chapters, or even finish one, but simply say, "Father, please speak exactly what I need right now." You may be amazed to find that it's only a few verses, maybe even only one verse, that will radically change the trajectory of your day. Don't limit the way that God wants to speak to you by forcing yourself to read too much, or too little. Study relationally and it will breathe a new life into your time with the Lord in His Word.

WORSHIP

I feel like I'm a little bit biased because I have the honor of leading people in worship on a weekly basis, but *I LOVE WORSHIP!* I'm obsessed with the thought of it, which can be a blessing and a curse because sometimes I think about it more than I practice it.

We've talked a lot about how worship is so much more than just singing songs in a corporate setting, but that it's something that we practice on a daily basis as we give our lives as sacrifices of praise to God. However, I do want to speak specifically about worship in terms of music.

I was raised around music. My dad is a stellar guitar player; I mean this guy can shred. So far as long as I can remember, music has always been in our home. Instruments were all over the place. He taught me drums when I was five years old, started showing me how to sing shortly after that, and guitar when I was eleven. Music was a huge part of our identity as a family.

I love almost every type of music. From classic rock to acoustic indie music, then from Christian hip hop to Johnny Cash, my musical tastes are like an all-you-can-eat buffet. Except country music...that's the one food this buffet doesn't serve! There are foods that resemble it, but no true country. I'm really sorry if that offends you. Please don't leave yet, we're almost finished.

With all the music that I love, nothing even begins to compare to the love that I have for worship music. The reason is that it transcends a musical preference because it actually taps into a calling and eternal destiny that each believer in Christ has upon their life. We were built for worship. We were built to join the song of the angels, "Holy, holy, holy, Lord God Almighty, who was and is and is to come!" (Revelation 4:8).

You might be a very reserved worshiper, or maybe you don't really let what's going on in your heart affect your physical posture. I'm not judging you at all. I definitely have those moments myself. I will say though, that if you're not moved by any of the content of worship music, if there's not a lyric that grips you, then please consider Christ's sacrifice for *you*.

This changed the way that I worshiped. When I realized that what God gave was a personal gift to me, wrapped in grace, it drew me to raise my hands in surrender. When I understood the sinful state that I was in as Jesus spoke forgiveness over me, it caused me to close my eyes in wondrous surrender.

There's no cookie-cutter way to worship the Lord, but there are many examples through scripture of how we can worship Him in spirit and truth. David danced before the Lord with all his might. Jehoshaphat sent out the worshipers before the army to fight the battle with praise, and God fought it for them. Mary spent time at Jesus' feet. Paul and Silas sang at midnight from prison until there was an earthquake and they were freed.

Worship accomplishes things in the spiritual realm that we may not understand until we're face to face with our Maker.

FELLOWSHIP

The body of Christ is an invaluable part of our walk with God. People can say all that they want that it's not necessary, but that's just not what we read in scripture. Hebrews 10:25 says, "And let us not neglect our meeting together, as some people do, but encourage one another, especially now that the day of his return is drawing near" (NLT).

I don't think we need very much more clarity on the point. Jesus is returning soon, so we must continue to gather together, and as iron sharpens iron we will strengthen each other in seasons when we are feeling weak.

The gift of community is one of the ways that the Lord continues to surprise me. It's amazing how He can bring people into your life at the perfect time. People will continue to point back to His truth and convey His heart in a way that you'll best understand it in that season.

If you aren't already, I highly encourage you to make fellowship a big part of your life. Simply put, we're better when we're together. I don't mean that we need to live in a Christian bubble, never being subjected to the world. If we did that, people would never hear about Jesus. We need to follow the commission to go out and make disciples, but we need to make sure that we have a strong community of believers who are supporting us in prayer and fellowship as we go out.

Jesus loved His church so much that He gave Himself for her. May we never neglect one of the gifts that Jesus has granted us by the shedding of His blood. Fellowship, as we know it, is only possible because of His Spirit that unifies us. Aside from the common bond of Christ, we're generally a bunch of people from different backgrounds who would never be friends outside of Christ, but because of Christ, we're able to be closer than family sometimes. What a precious gift it is.

CHAPTER SEVENTEEN:
LIVE RELATIONALLY

You did it! You made it through the book. I hope that the Lord has ministered to you and somehow revealed more of His heart for you.

I'm reminded how Moses met with God on the top of the mountain, and when he came back down, his face was shining like the sun. Mo was radiant, so much so that he covered his face with a veil to conceal the glory.

In a similar way, when you walk with God in a relational way as His child, there will be a noticeable difference in your life. You will become a person that people will desire to be around, simply because of the One who you've been around.

Being a child of God is cool because it's a family that you get to invite others to be a part of.

When people notice the difference in your countenance, invite them to a family get-together—church! If they ask why you have so much joy, share a story with them—your testimony! Living for Jesus can be a fun adventure. Live relationally with your Father, and with people, and watch Him transform the way you live out the rest of your days until you see Him face to face.

ACKNOWLEDGEMENTS

Thank you, Dad and Mom, for showing me the heart of our heavenly Father through the way that you loved Amanda and me growing up. I'm truly blessed to have such amazing parents. I love you!

This book would have never been written if it weren't for the loving prodding from one of my best friends in the world, Erik Sahakian. Thank you, my brother, for years of meaningful friendship and the wisdom you've imparted—I love you.

Thank you, Rolly Ladd, for supporting every project I've done. I am so grateful for you!

Thank you to the pastors at Wildwood: Pastor Chris, Jason, Erik, Matt, Jake, Zach, Phil, Mike, and Kenny. I love you all and I am so grateful for your friendships and godly influence.

Thank you to the friends who have become family to us: Brian and Rosie, Justin and Sarah, and Jon and Krystin. You have all shown my family what true community is like, and I cannot thank you enough for the gift that each of you have been to us.

Thank you, Dave Rolph, for pouring into my life at such a young age and showing me what a true man of God in ministry looks like. I love you!